Young Explorers

AROUND

NEW YORK

Text by Daniela Celli

Illustrations by Laura Re

DEAR PARENTS...

You may be wondering why you should take your children to a chaotic and noisy city
that is entangled in a ball of steel cobwebs, where the air smells not
of the ocean but of hot dogs and construction.
The answer is simple: There is no corner of this city that does not have a story to tell;
every street, skyscraper, and park has something to discover.
New York is a huge playground where you can experience the most extraordinary
adventures: walk along old railway tracks, fly above the skyscrapers to an island
with a lighthouse, rent a rowboat, climb excitedly up a terrace,
or witness the most beautiful of sunsets while on a century-old wooden steed.
This is New York, as Miroslav Sasek would say.
This guide aims to be a small, child-friendly resource of places, stories, and curiosities,
to be used when reading on the sofa or when actually traveling.
I included some of the things I discovered when New York was my city
and some others that my kids loved every time we went back.
I hope that it will be an invitation to your children to discover the world, too,
with curiosity and with eyes always full of amazement and wonder!

To Charlie, with all the love in the world.
Now run happy on carpets of clouds.

Daniela Celli

GOOD MORNING, YOUNG EXPLORERS!

My name is Mr. Squirrel, and I live in a big tree along a somewhat wild path
in Central Park, but I love traveling around New York City to discover the stories
and curiosities that it hides.
For example, I've heard that there may be a treasure hidden under a stone
on Liberty Island, and I know for sure that there is a huge Titanosaur skeleton
at the Natural History Museum!
Why don't you come with me?

I had a lot of fun preparing four different itineraries for you so that
we can explore some of the most famous places in this unique city.
Where else is an ice hockey rink transformed in minutes into a basketball
court? Each route begins with a map of all the planned stops.
And in between one fun fact and another, you will also find some
games, so please keep your eyes peeled!
Are you ready?

LET'S GO ON
AN ADVENTURE!

ITINERARIES

NEW YORK

Good morning, kids, and welcome to New York City!

AMERICAN MUSEUM OF NATURAL HISTORY

2

1

CENTRAL PARK

HUDSON RIVER

BROADWAY

3 METROPOLITAN MUSEUM OF ART

ROOSEVELT ISLAND TRAMWAY

4

ITINERARY 1

Today we'll begin exploring the city, starting with some of the main landmarks of *Upper Manhattan*, the area that stretches across one side of Central Park to the other. We will go hunting for statues, we will get lost among the fossils and the works of art at two extraordinary museums, and finally, we will sail over the city aboard a flying tram.

EAST RIVER

• Almost impossible to get lost

Manhattan was designed as if it were a giant chess board.

The *AVENUES* are the wide roads that cut it vertically, numbered in ascending order from east to west. The *STREETS* are the roads that divide the city horizontally and grow in number from south to north. *Broadway* is the only street that crosses it diagonally!

• The city on an island

The name *Manhattan* comes from the word *manaháhtaan* and means THE PLACE TO FIND WOOD TO MAKE BOWS in *Lenape*, the language of the Indigenous people who inhabited it before the arrival of the settlers. What is now a city dotted with skyscrapers was once a hilly area full of forests and lakes, inhabited by bears and eagles.

CENTRAL PARK

Welcome to New York's Greatest Park!

More than 2.5 miles (4 km) long and 0.5 mile (800 m) wide, Central Park is the great green lung of Manhattan. It contains artificial lakes, statues, fountains, beautiful playgrounds, a castle, a zoo, and even a puppet theater. You can walk, go boating, run, bike, and of course have a nice picnic. In summer you can attend shows and concerts, while from October to March there is a fantastic ice skating rink.

• Welcome to my house

Are you curious to know where I live? Then you just need to go to *the Ramble*, an area of enchanting pathways with a slightly wild appearance that is home to numerous little animals: other squirrels like me, birds, chipmunks, opossums, turtles, and many raccoons who love to sleep in the branches of the trees.
HOW MANY CAN YOU SPOT? AFTER YOU HAVE FOUND THEM ALL, PLAY WITH THE STATUES IN THE PARK!

• Alice in Wonderland

Sitting on a giant mushroom, Alice is surrounded by the other famous characters of Lewis Carroll's beloved novel: the Cheshire Cat, the White Rabbit, the Dormouse and...who else do you recognize?

It's the Mad Hatter!

• A four-legged hero

In 1925 a group of brave sled dogs, including BALTO, traveled hundreds of miles through the Alaskan ice, facing dangers and snowstorms, to carry medicine that would save the lives of many people. The Siberian husky statue is dedicated to Balto and the other four-legged heroes.

AND NOW HOW ABOUT VISITING A MUSEUM? For NATURAL HISTORY turn the page; if you prefer ART instead, go to page 12. BOTH ARE JUST OUTSIDE CENTRAL PARK!

AMERICAN MUSEUM OF NATURAL HISTORY

One could spend a whole week here
and still not be able to see it all.

Oh yes, the American Museum of Natural History in New York is the largest museum of its kind in the world! Spread over five floors, including the basement, history, nature, science, and culture appear in the form of dioramas, reconstructions, fossils, and scenographic installations divided into 45 huge thematic rooms.

APPARENTLY IT CONTAINS OVER 33 MILLION SPECIMENS!

• A night at the museum
The famous film *Night at the Museum* is set here. Ben Stiller plays the role of Larry, a night watchman who discovers that an ancient Egyptian tablet has the power to bring everything in the museum to life...

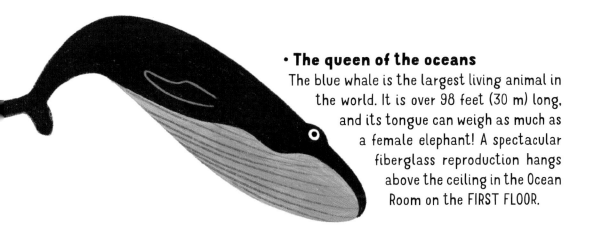

• The queen of the oceans

The blue whale is the largest living animal in the world. It is over 98 feet (30 m) long, and its tongue can weigh as much as a female elephant! A spectacular fiberglass reproduction hangs above the ceiling in the Ocean Room on the FIRST FLOOR.

• The giant of Patagonia

On the FOURTH FLOOR in a magnificent exhibit dedicated to fossils is the life-size reproduction of the skeleton of a Titanosaur, a huge dinosaur discovered in Patagonia in 2014. This gigantic sauroped with a very long neck weighed as much as thirteen elephants and was as long as three buses.

LUCKILY IT WAS AN HERBIVORE!

• From space to Earth

On the FIRST FLOOR you can experience the thrill of touching the Willamette meteorite, the largest meteorite ever found in the United States. DOESN'T IT LOOK LIKE A GIANT CHUNK OF SWISS CHEESE? The craters in it are due to the erosion caused on Earth by atmospheric agents. Indeed, the huge piece of iron landed on our planet thousands of years ago, after traveling at a speed of 40,000 miles (64,000 km) per hour.

METROPOLITAN MUSEUM OF ART

Have you ever played time travel?

Visiting the MET is a bit like taking a journey through history. You get a map of the museum, choose the period, the place, and what you'd like to see, and POOF! You can jump from the Classical era to the twentieth century. WITH OVER TWO MILLION WORKS OF ART, THE MET IS ONE OF THE LARGEST ART MUSEUMS IN THE WORLD.

• Fearless warriors

Are you fascinated by the world of knights? On the first floor you will find yourself in front of a real parade of paladins on horseback. The armor section includes pieces from around the world that belonged to princes, kings, and even Japanese samurai.

• The time of the pharaohs

Do you have a passion for ancient Egypt? The EGYPTIAN EXHIBIT hosts the wonderful *TEMPLE OF DENDUR!* Just think...in order to transport the very heavy blocks of stone here, 661 cases had to travel by sea aboard a large cargo ship.

• Art in the open air

Even the roof of the MET hosts different works of art every year. On the rooftop, you can also have a drink or eat a snack at the bar, enjoying a magnificent view of the surrounding skyscrapers!

If you like art, within walking distance of the MET are two other splendid museums: the *GUGGENHEIM MUSEUM*, dedicated to modern and contemporary art, and the *MOMA*, the Museum of Modern Art.

ROOSEVELT ISLAND TRAMWAY

Ready to fly over the city?

Don't worry, I'm not crazy! We squirrels make big leaps but we don't get that far! To reach *Roosevelt Island* we have to get on one of the two red trams that carry up to 110 people at a time from Manhattan.

TO GET TO THE ISLAND, THE TRAM TAKES ONLY FOUR MINUTES, AND THE VIEW IS SPECTACULAR!

• The little apple from New York

Roosevelt Island is a small island about 1.8 miles (3 km) long, located in the middle of the East River between *Manhattan* and *Queens*. It once housed hospitals, prisons, and asylums, but today it is a quiet residential place where you can stroll along the river, enjoying a magnificent view of the city. On the northern tip there is an old stone lighthouse from the 1800s.

HOW ABOUT RENTING A BIKE AND RIDING THERE?

• Saved by a superhero!
In 2002 the tram was featured in a breathtaking scene in the film *Spider-Man*.

In the film, Spider-Man is forced by the Green Goblin to decide whether to save Mary Jane, who is hanging from the Queensboro Bridge, or the passengers of the tram. HOW DO YOU THINK IT ENDED?

Seek and find
A red bicycle, a cat, 2 rowboats, a fisherman, a man in a striped sweater, 7 seagulls, 3 families of ducks, and a dog.

15

Hello, kids! Ready to go?

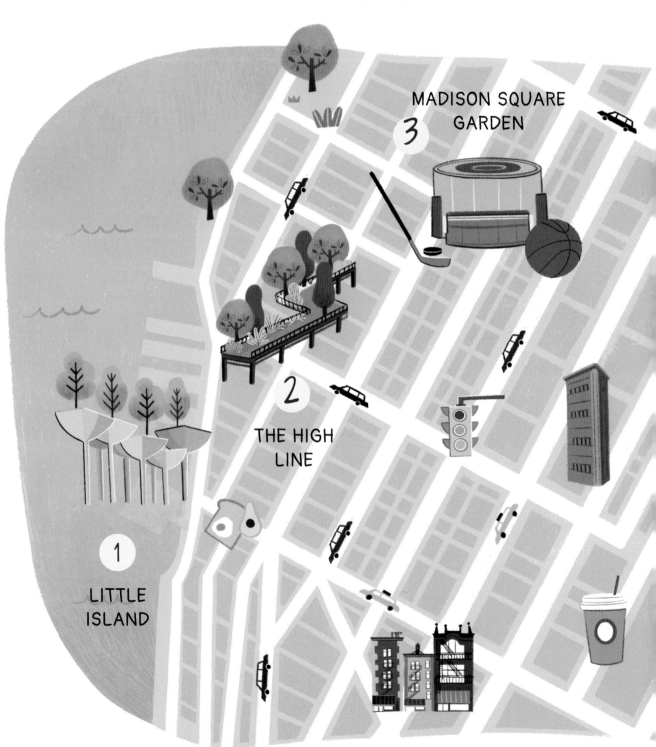

3 MADISON SQUARE GARDEN

2 THE HIGH LINE

1 LITTLE ISLAND

ITINERARY 2

Today's adventure will take us around some of the most famous places in Midtown, the heart of Manhattan, and we're also going to discover two extraordinary GREEN AREAS, one suspended in the sky and the other sitting over the Hudson River. We will climb two very tall SKYSCRAPERS and discover the secrets of one of the most famous ARENAS in the world. *Saddle up*, let's go!

4

CHRYSLER BUILDING

5

EMPIRE STATE BUILDING

• Outdoor showers

There are over 100,000 fire hydrants in New York today. The first was installed in 1808, in order to replace the buckets of water left around in case of fire.

In the heat of the summer, residents of northern Manhattan and the Bronx can exploit this resource to...cool off. But first, you have to go to a fire station with an adult and ask for a special spray cap. Otherwise you will pay a hefty fine!

• A hot dog, please

You can't walk through Manhattan without eating at least one hot dog, sold from carts on practically every street corner. There are numerous legends about how the hot dog got its name, but we know for sure that the "dog" is a dachshund, whose shape resembles that of a sausage.

LITTLE ISLAND

Follow me to Little Island! Today we are going to discover the extraordinary "floating" island on the Hudson River.

Do you see those gigantic tulip-shaped pylons in the water, like flowers suspended on the river? There are 132 of them, and all together they are part of a magnificent park of 2.4 acres (1 hectare), bigger than a football field! You can get there by crossing one of the two pedestrian bridges and then walking from one side to the other because all the "flowers" are connected to each other.

I love climbing the trees and playing peek-a-boo with views of skyscrapers. DID YOU KNOW THAT YOU CAN ALSO SEE THE STATUE OF LIBERTY FROM HERE?

• The calm after the storm
Little Island was built in 2021 on top of the old Pier 54 that ten years earlier had been severely damaged by Hurricane Sandy. In addition to beautiful plants and many flowers, this oasis of peace has two open-air theaters and an area dedicated to food trucks.

HOW ABOUT A PICNIC? I HAVE A SOFT SPOT FOR AVOCADO TOAST! YUMMY!

• The remains of an important past
At the foot of South Bridge is a giant steel arch. It is all that remains of what was once the place for the great ocean liners, such as the LUSITANIA and the TITANIC, to depart and arrive. Unfortunately the latter never reached the dock because it sank after colliding with an *ICEBERG!*

THE HIGH LINE

Come on young explorers, follow me up the
stairs. We are about to go to a park where once
upon a time trains ran!

• In the beginning...

In the second half of the 19th century, Manhattan was crossed by a railway
network that connected the central station to downtown. LONG PUFFING TRAINS
whizzed along the tracks in the middle of the city and, as you can imagine,
the risk of accidents was very high. To solve the problem, a few swashbuckling
horsemen were employed to gallop up and down between the rails waving a red
flag every time a train passed! AND IT WENT ON LIKE THIS UNTIL 1935, WHEN THEY
HAD THE INGENIOUS IDEA OF RAISING THE RAILWAY.

... later on...

The emergence of other types of transportation decreased the demand
for trains, and by 1980 the tracks became a GHOST RAILWAY. Plants and
vegetation grew around the rails, turning it into a true URBAN JUNGLE for
almost 30 years, until a residents' association had another brilliant idea:
WHY NOT TURN IT INTO A PARK?

... and finally, today

The High Line is a linear park that "flies" between the buildings for 1.45 miles (2.3 km). It's a very long SECRET GARDEN where plants, flowers, and trees stretch between the buildings above the city traffic. There are also fountains, artwork, park benches, and even cafés and restaurants!

MADISON SQUARE GARDEN

Ready to visit one of the most famous sports arenas in the world?

In addition to being home to the famous NEW YORK KNICKS basketball team and the NEW YORK RANGERS hockey team, Madison Square Garden hosts countless sporting events each year as well as popular shows and concerts. The large circular building, built in 1968 on the site of an old train station, can accommodate 20,000 people.

ITS NAME IS A TRIBUTE TO JAMES MADISON, FOURTH PRESIDENT OF THE UNITED STATES.

• A magical floor

Sometimes, on the same day, ice hockey is played in the afternoon and basketball in the evening.

SO WHAT HAPPENS TO THE ICE?
After the hockey game, the frozen rink is first covered with special plywood and then with the parquet of the basketball court, assembled like a jigsaw puzzle, piece by piece.

• Superstition

Rituals and even superstitious habits are quite common among NBA players: There are those who stroke their right cheek three times before throwing the ball, those who hum while doing a dance, those who throw a kiss to the sky, and even those who eat a peanut butter and jelly sandwich an hour before every game!

Seek and find

A man with a mustache and a hat, a boy in a striped shirt, Willy The Squirrel, a woman eating popcorn, a girl with red curly hair, and twin boys.

CHRYSLER BUILDING

Hey friends, can you see me?

Opened in 1929, the Chrysler Building earned the title of tallest skyscraper in the world thanks to an ingenious ploy: the last-minute addition of a spire built in great secrecy that, along with a mighty flagpole, raised it to the top height of 1,046 feet (318.90 m), beating competing buildings.

• A "cumbersome" structure

Born as the headquarters of the famous car manufacturer Chrysler, the structure is inspired by the world of machines. Parts of this beautiful skyscraper consist of none other than stylized cars, hubcaps, fenders, and radiator caps! DO YOU SEE THE GARGOYLES ON THE 61ST FLOOR? I'm on one of them! If you look closely you will realize that it is not just any monster, but an eagle similar to the hood ornaments on Chrysler's Plymouth cars.

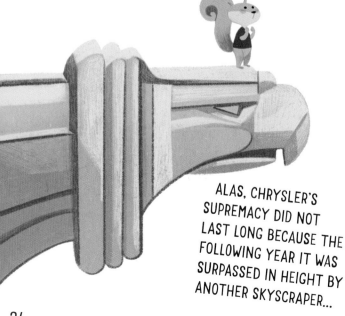

ALAS, CHRYSLER'S SUPREMACY DID NOT LAST LONG BECAUSE THE FOLLOWING YEAR IT WAS SURPASSED IN HEIGHT BY ANOTHER SKYSCRAPER...

EMPIRE STATE BUILDING

Here's who stole the record from Chrysler!

Built in just 410 days, the Empire State Building was inaugurated in 1931 and immediately became a symbol of New York and of America itself. With its dizzying height of 1,453 feet (443 m), it took the record of tallest skyscraper in the world from the Chrysler Building, which had kept the title for only one year.

• Light displays

When darkness falls on the Big Apple, the top thirty floors of the building are illuminated with colored lights that change for special events and holidays. For example, it's red and green for Christmas and orange and black for Halloween!

• Run Up

Every year the Empire State Building is home to a truly unique race. To win, participants must reach the 86th floor as quickly as possible. The most agile runners manage to climb the 1,576 steps in less than ten minutes!

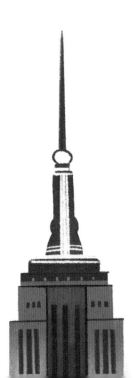

I PREFER TO USE THE ELEVATOR!

WALKING WITH YOUR NOSE UP:
LET'S DISCOVER SOME OTHER SKYSCRAPERS

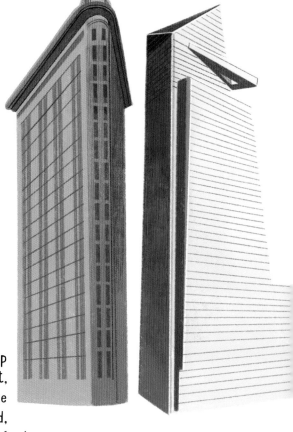

• Flatiron Bulding
A strange iron

With a height of "only" 285 feet (87 m) it is certainly not among the tallest skyscrapers in New York, but it is one of the most unusual. Many were convinced that such a narrow building would collapse at the first gust of wind. But they were wrong!

DUE TO ITS BIZARRE SHAPE IT WAS FIRST NICKNAMED "SLICE OF CAKE" AND THEN "IRON," A NAME THAT STILL REMAINS TODAY!

• 30 Hudson Yards
Only for the brave!

It takes a good deal of courage to climb up to the 100th floor of 30 Hudson Yards. In fact, it is here that *The Edge* is located, one of the highest outdoor viewing platforms in the world, suspended in the void and with a floor of glass.

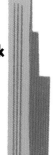

One World Trade Center
1,776 feet
(541 m)

Central Park Tower
1,550 feet
(472 m)

Steinway Tower
1,428 feet
(435 m)

One Vanderbilt
1,400 feet
(427 m)

DID YOU KNOW THAT
THERE ARE MORE THAN
6,400 HIGH-RISE BUILDINGS
IN NEW YORK????

• Steinway Tower

The skinniest

The Steinway Tower is the thinnest skyscraper in the world, so much so that looking at it one has the sensation that the building disappears in the clouds because the depth decreases with the height.

Inside there are luxury apartments that share a gym, a swimming pool, and even a tennis court!

• One World Trade Center

Never forget

One World Trade Center, also called the Freedom Tower, is the tallest skyscraper in New York and in the United States. Its construction began a few years after a terrible attack brought down the Twin Towers. The new building stands right next to Ground Zero, the area where the two destroyed buildings were located and which today houses a beautiful memorial, as well as a museum dedicated to the sad events that took place on September 11, 2001.

432 Park Avenue
1,397 feet
(426 m)

Empire State Building
1,454 feet
(443 m)

30 Hudson Yards
1,296 feet
(395 m)

Bank of America Tower
1,200 feet
(366 m)

My dear kids, a new adventure awaits us!

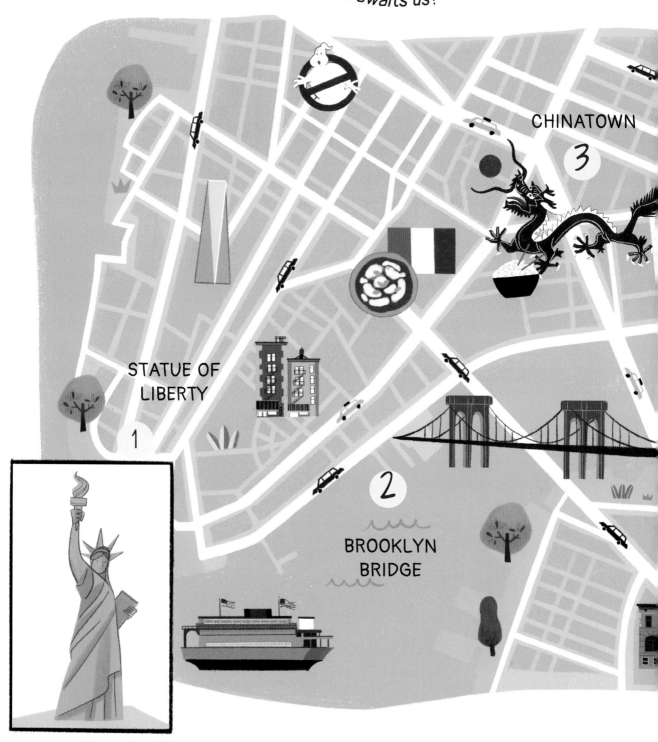

CHINATOWN

3

STATUE OF
LIBERTY

1

2

BROOKLYN
BRIDGE

ITINERARY 3

The third itinerary begins onboard a boat that will take us to one of the most famous monuments in the world. Once back on land we will walk across an extraordinary suspension bridge, and finally we will go to...China! IMPOSSIBLE?
Nothing is impossible in New York!
Come on!

• The ghost barracks
There is no corner of this city that hasn't appeared in a movie. Just think, at least 150 movies are filmed here every year! Among the many sets that can be visited, not far from Chinatown in Tribeca, there is a very special fire station.
In 1984 it was the headquarters for a friendly group of GHOSTBUSTERS!

IF YOU GO, LOOK FOR THE GHOST ON THE SIDEWALK!

• Little Italy and Mulberry Street
Beginning in the mid-19th century, thousands of Italians came to live in New York.
Most of them settled in an area of Lower Manhattan that later came to be known as Little Italy. Today, not that much remains of Little Italy, except a street full of restaurants, pizzerias, and old-fashioned Italian music.

STATUE OF LIBERTY

All abooooaaaaard!

To reach the Statue of Liberty, one of the most famous monuments in the world, we have to take a boat that travels from the tip of Manhattan to Liberty Island in just 15 minutes. Once disembarked, you may decide to climb the steep spiral stairs to get up to the crown.

AS LONG AS YOU ARE NOT AFRAID OF HEIGHTS!

• From France with friendship

The Statue of Liberty was built in France by sculptor *Frédéric-Auguste Bartholdi* in collaboration with *Gustave Eiffel*—yes, the famous builder of the Eiffel Tower. It was then "cut into pieces" and placed in 214 crates, which were loaded onto a ship to be transported to America. During the crossing, the frigate faced a severe storm, but after 27 days, it arrived in New York safely.

• A change of clothes

When it was unveiled in 1886, the "skin" of the statue was reddish-brown. Over the years, the copper with which it is coated has oxidized, giving it its current green color.

• An important detail

Look at the feet of the statue.
WHAT DO YOU NOTICE? They are gigantic!
If Lady Liberty had to buy more sandals,
she would need size 879!

BROOKLYN BRIDGE

Let's go back to the mainland (almost...) to cross
one of the most charming bridges in New York!

Completed in 1883, the Brooklyn Bridge was the largest suspension bridge in the world for several years. To build its mammoth steel structure, 600 workers faced the unspeakable risk of diving into underwater excavation chambers to work on the foundations.

Just under 1.2 miles (2 km) long, it crosses the East River, connecting Manhattan with Brooklyn. Cars drive on the lower part while the upper area can be covered on foot or by bicycle.

• Feathery neighbors

Please, stay close to me while we cross it. I'm a bit scared because peregrine falcons build their nests right on the bridge towers. HOW MANY CAN YOU SPOT? *HELP!*

• Elephant-proof

Some unfortunate events and tragic accidents that occurred before and after the opening of the bridge caused widespread fear among citizens, who did not believe in its stability.

P.T. Barnum, the famous founder of the Barnum and Bailey Circus, disproved these fears by demonstrating the solidity of the structure and at the same time getting publicity.

ON MAY 17, 1884, HE CROSSED THE BROOKLYN BRIDGE WITH 21 ELEPHANTS, 10 CAMELS, AND 7 DROMEDARIES.

CHINATOWN

Shall we go to China? *No, my friends, I'm not going crazy!*
Anything is possible in New York!

Many different cultures coexist in New York, inherited from the populations that have moved here from all over the world. Today we're going to discover Chinatown, the fascinatingly colorful, crowded, and tasty Chinese district!

• Unusual tastes

According to historians, it seems that ice cream was born in Asia. SO HOW ABOUT TRYING SOME?

The *Ice Cream Factory*, with its characteristic sign, has been producing ice cream for over forty years.

Among the most unusual ice cream flavors, you can choose RED BEAN, PANDAN plant, and TARO, a tuber that is similar to a potato, only purple!

• **Yùnhóng Chopsticks**
HAVE YOU EVER TRIED EATING WITH TWO STICKS?
Since ancient times in China, chopsticks have been used instead of forks! At 50 Mott Street you can buy all kinds of chopsticks. Some are decorated with drawings that illustrate a story, a brief poem, or even animals.

WHO KNOWS? THE SQUIRREL MIGHT BE THERE TOO!

Seek and find
A lucky fortune cat, a lucky bamboo plant, 4 bowls of rice, 2 fans, a Chinese chessboard, and Mr. Squirrel.

35

OTHER AREAS

• Little Red Lighthouse
(Fort Washington Park, Upper Manhattan)
Overlooking the Hudson River is a small, squat, cute red lighthouse, the only one in Manhattan.

It's been there since before the George Washington Bridge was built in 1931, and up until then it had directed sailors. The bridge's new lighting system rendered the lighthouse useless, and a few years later the Coast Guard planned to auction it off.

Fortunately, thanks to the writer Hildegarde H. Swift writing a book about it and because of protests by people who were fond of it, the Little Red Lighthouse was saved and still stands today.

• Jane's Carousel
(DUMBO)
There is no carousel with a better view than the one in beautiful Brooklyn Bridge Park. The old carousel, which recently turned 100, was built in 1922 and was originally installed in Ohio. Ruined by time, it was about to be sold piece by piece, but in 1983 it was bought by a couple of artists, Jane and David Walentas.

The 48 horses were lovingly restored, and they now give happiness to all children who visit DUMBO, the neighborhood "down under the Manhattan Bridge overpass."

• Coney Island

(Brooklyn)

At the southern end of Brooklyn there is a small peninsula where not only was the hot dog allegedly invented, but a world-famous amusement park, called Luna Park, was first opened in 1903.

In addition to taking a dip in the ocean, a ride on the 100-year-old Ferris wheel is a must. The Wonder Wheel is 150 feet (45 m) high, and it has red and blue cars that swing, while the white ones stay still.

WHICH CAR
WOULD YOU
CHOOSE?

I can't believe we've reached the last itinerary!

Aladdin

2
BROADWAY

3
ROCKEFELLER
CENTER

TIMES
SQUARE

1

4
NEW YORK
PUBLIC
LIBRARY

ITINERARY 4

Today will be full of fantastic places and interesting stories. We will start from a square in the shape of a bowtie, we will discover the set of a famous film where the young protagonist misses his plane, we will go to find the Kings of the public library, and we will end our journey in a SPECIAL STATION.

Hurry up, let's go!

GRAND CENTRAL TERMINAL

5

• Stage on wheels

One of the most popular ways of getting around New York is the subway. With almost 500 stations and over 620 miles (1,000 km) of tracks, it allows you to easily reach every corner of the Big Apple. The subway cars and stations are also the stage for many street artists who entertain passengers by playing instruments, singing, and even performing acrobatic acts!

• Lost and Found

Forgot something on the train? Don't worry! At Grand Central Terminal there is a special office that collects and catalogs whatever is left on trains. Among the most unusual findings are several wedding dresses, a karaoke machine, engagement rings, and even a fake leg!

TIMES SQUARE/BROADWAY

Welcome to the loudest, most chaotic, glittering, and glamorous neighborhood in New York!

Time Square, which owes its name to the famous American newspaper the *New York Times*, is a riot of skyscrapers topped by gigantic neon signs and billboards up to seven floors high! Despite the unusual shape, similar to a large bowtie, it is officially a square, one of the busiest in the world!

• A show for extraterrestrials

As seen in images taken by the Mission 16 crew, Times Square is so bright that it's easily visible from space.

• New Year's Eve

For over a century, on December 31 each year, Times Square has been filled with hundreds of thousands of people who come here to celebrate the New Year.

FOR THE OCCASION, A LARGE CRYSTAL BALL ILLUMINATED BY 32,000 LED LIGHTS IS SENT DOWN THE POLE OF A SKYSCRAPER AND, AT THE STROKE OF MIDNIGHT A TON OF CONFETTI IS RELEASED OVER THE CROWD!

• A "show-off" road

Time Square is crossed by Broadway, one of the oldest streets in the city and the first to be lit by gas lamps. Approximately 31 miles (50 km) long, it is known for the Theater District, with more than forty theaters!

SOME OF THE MOST FAMOUS MUSICALS HAVE INCLUDED *THE PHANTOM OF THE OPERA, CATS, ALADDIN, THE LION KING,* AND *FROZEN!*

WOULD YOU LIKE TO SEE A SHOW?

ROCKEFELLER CENTER

Ready to sharpen your skate blades?

In 1930 *John Rockefeller Jr.*, the son of the richest man in the world, built a huge complex of buildings in Midtown. Today the 19 buildings, connected by long shopping arcades, include theaters, television studios, the spectacular panoramic terrace Top of the Rock, and, from November to March, one of the most FAMOUS ICE-SKATING RINKS IN THE WORLD!

• *So This Is Christmas*

It really isn't Christmas in New York until the Rockefeller Center tree lights up!
For almost a century, a giant spruce tree has been placed in Rockefeller Plaza in late November. The tree is illuminated by over 45,000 lights, and a large Swarovski star made up of over 25,000 crystals dominates the top! *WOW!*

• **Have you ever see *Home Alone*?**

In this famous Christmas film, after many misadventures, Kevin hugs his mother right here.

NEW YORK PUBLIC LIBRARY

Help! Stay close to me, kids, those two beasts scare me!

Outside the beautiful building that houses one of the largest libraries in the United States, there is a large staircase where two imposing marble lions have stood guard since 1911. The two animals are so loved by New Yorkers that in addition to becoming the protagonists of a book, they are also the mascots of the library!

• Lion or beaver?
Not everyone agreed with the decision to put two lions in front of the library. There were those who, like President Teddy Roosevelt, would have preferred two bison, and those who would have preferred two enormous beavers! Before being called Patience and Fortitude the two animals' names were changed several times.

WHAT NAMES WOULD YOU HAVE CHOSEN?

GRAND CENTRAL TERMINAL

Raise your hand if you are fascinated by stations and trains!

In addition to being the largest station in the world, Grand Central Terminal is a place full of stories and interesting facts, starting with why it was built. In 1902, the collision of two steam trains accelerated the idea of expanding the use of electric trains, which were safer and less polluting. Therefore, a new station was built in place of the old one.

• A ceiling full of wonders
Do you know what the first thing is that you have to do when you enter the station?
Look up!

THE CEILING IS PAINTED AS IF IT WERE AN IMMENSE NIGHT SKY COVERED WITH ZODIAC SIGNS AND 2,500 STARS, SOME OF WHICH ARE ILLUMINATED BY LED LIGHTS!

• *The Whispering Gallery*
On the second basement floor, in front of the Oyster Bar, is a very special gallery.

IF YOU STAND UNDER THE FIRST ARCH AND WHISPER SOMETHING, THE PERSON ON THE OPPOSITE SIDE CAN HEAR YOU, DUE TO A SPECIAL ACOUSTIC EFFECT. GIVE IT A TRY!

• Smart clocks
All of Grand Central Terminal's clocks are set exactly one minute ahead. This reduces the risk of passengers missing their train!

Seek and find

A suitcase covered in stickers, a guitar case, a green backpack, a small brown suitcase, a little dog.

45

URBAN LEGENDS

My dear friends, we have seen many things so far, but New York is good at hiding many others—things that nobody has ever proven to be real but that everyone talks about...

• Alligators in the sewers

One day some kids bought baby alligators with the idea of keeping them as pets. But when the poor reptiles grew a little, they were flushed down the drain. Although this story seems unlikely, it is said that there have been numerous sightings of big green "monsters" in the sewers of New York.

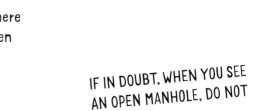

IF IN DOUBT, WHEN YOU SEE AN OPEN MANHOLE, DO NOT GO NEAR IT!

• A ghost ship

Looking at the Hudson River on a foggy day, you might see an unusual vessel floating on the surface of the water. If you do, don't worry: it's just the ghost of a vessel that was wrecked here a few centuries ago.

• A dangerous treasure

Before being hanged for piracy in 1701, Captain William Kidd is said to have hid his treasure under a large flat rock on Liberty Island. Before you go digging, you should know that those who have tried to find it have found an unpleasant surprise. It seems that a fearsome ghost with a saber is watching over the gold.

BETTER NOT TAKE ANY RISKS!

• The ghost sisters

If you feel like ice skating while walking through Central Park in the winter, you might find yourself whizzing side by side with sisters Janet and Rosetta Van Der Voort. But don't worry if they are faster than you: by observing the skates you will notice that...THEY DON'T TOUCH THE GROUND!

MY DEAR EXPLORERS WE HAVE REACHED THE END OF OUR JOURNEY! I HOPE YOU ENJOYED THIS ADVENTURE AND THAT ALL THE THINGS YOU SAW AND LEARNED WILL SOON TURN INTO TREASURED MEMORIES.

GOODBYE, MY FRIENDS!

LAURA RE

Born in Rome, Laura attended the Roman School of Comics. She has collaborated with animation studios as a character designer, concept artist, and illustrator. After attending the International School of Illustration of Sàrmede, she moved to Milan to obtain a master's degree in illustration of Mimaster. Here she deepened her knowledge of publishing and of illustrations for children.

DANIELA CELLI

Daniela was born in Florence in 1977. After studying piano at the Luigi Cherubini Conservatory, she moved to New York, where she began studying criminology. In 1997 she returned to Italy, graduated in law, and also obtained a diploma from the Academy of Dramatic Arts. Always passionate about travel, since 2008 she has been blogging about adventures with her family around the world.

Graphic layout: Valentina Figus

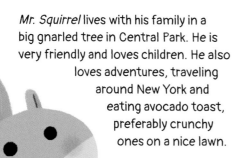

Mr. Squirrel lives with his family in a big gnarled tree in Central Park. He is very friendly and loves children. He also loves adventures, traveling around New York and eating avocado toast, preferably crunchy ones on a nice lawn.

WHITE STAR KIDS

White Star Kids™ is a trademark of White Star s.r.l.

© 2023 White Star s.r.l.
Piazzale Luigi Cadorna, 6
20123 Milan, Italy
www.whitestar.it

Translation: Inga Sempel
Editing: Michele Suchomel-Casey

First printing, June 2023

ISBN 978-88-544-1994-0
1 2 3 4 5 6   27 26 25 24 23

Printed and manufactured
in Slovenia by DZS Grafik

MIX
Paper from responsible sources
FSC® C178000